GRAPHIC MODERN HISTORY: WORLD WAR II

THE WESTERN FRONT

By Gary Jeffrey & Illustrated by Terry Riley

Crabtree Publishing Company

www.crabtreebooks.com

SOMERSET CO. LIBRARY
BRIDGEWATER, N.J. 08807

Crabtree Publishing Company

www.crabtreebooks.com

Created and produced by:
David West Children's Books

Project development, design, and concept:
David West Children's Books

Author and designer: Gary Jeffrey

Illustrator: Terry Riley

Editor: Lynn Peppas

Proofreader: Wendy Scavuzzo

Project coordinator: Kathy Middleton

Production and print coordinator:
Katherine Berti

Prepress technician: Katherine Berti

Photographs:
Bundesarchiv: pages 4b, 5t Jule Rouard
(scan Luc Viatour): page 44b City of
Westminster Archives Centre: page 47b

Library and Archives Canada Cataloguing in Publication

CIP available at Library and Archives Canada

Library of Congress Cataloging-in-Publication Data

Jeffrey, Gary.
The western front / Gary Jeffrey ; & illustrated by Terry Riley.
p. cm. -- (Graphic modern history--World War II)
Includes index.
ISBN 978-0-7787-4196-1 (reinforced library binding : alk.
paper) -- ISBN 978-0-7787-4203-6 (pbk. : alk. paper) -- ISBN
978-1-4271-7876-3 (electronic pdf) -- ISBN 978-1-4271-7991-3
(electronic html)
1. World War, 1939-1945--Europe--Comic books, strips, etc. 2.
World War, 1939-1945--Europe--Juvenile literature. 3. Europe--
History--1918-1945--Comic books, strips, etc.. 4. Europe--
History--1918-1945--Juvenile literature. 5. Graphic novels. I.
Riley, Terry, ill. II. Title.

D743.7.J44 2012
940.54'21--dc23

2011050087

Crabtree Publishing Company

www.crabtreebooks.com   1-800-387-7650

Printed in Canada/012012/MA20111130

Copyright © **2012 CRABTREE PUBLISHING COMPANY**. All rights reserved. No part of this publication may be
reproduced, stored in a retrieval system or be transmitted in any form or by any means, electronic, mechanical, photocopying,
recording, or otherwise, without the prior written permission of Crabtree Publishing Company.

Published in Canada
Crabtree Publishing
616 Welland Ave.
St. Catharines, Ontario
L2M 5V6

Published in the United States
Crabtree Publishing
PMB 59051
350 Fifth Avenue, 59th Floor
New York, New York 10118

Published in the United Kingdom
Crabtree Publishing
Maritime House
Basin Road North, Hove
BN41 1WR

Published in Australia
Crabtree Publishing
3 Charles Street
Coburg North
VIC 3058

CONTENTS

EUROPE CRUSHED   4

D-DAY   6

JOHN BENTLEY-BEARD
DUEL IN THE SKIES—
THE BATTLE OF BRITAIN
SEPTEMBER 27, 1940   8

HAROLD BAUMGARTEN
SURVIVING OMAHA
BEACH—D-DAY
JUNE 6, 1944   20

ALEXANDER A. DRABIK
CAPTURING THE BRIDGE
AT REMAGEN—THE
INVASION OF GERMANY
MARCH 7, 1945   28

VICTORY IN EUROPE   44

GLOSSARY   46
INDEX   48

EUROPE CRUSHED

From the first moment he came to power, Adolf Hitler's overriding ambition was to expand Germany eastward into Russia. In March 1938, he annexed Austria. A year later, he invaded Czechoslovakia. Germany's next target was its large eastern neighbor, Poland. His generals argued for time to build a war machine, but Hitler gambled that western Europe would do nothing, just as they had throughout the 1930s.

Hitler was bent on gaining "Lebensraum" or "living space." Hitler wanted more room for Germans in Europe.

Poland was a territory that both Germany and Russia felt entitled to.

BLITZKRIEG

Alarmed by German aims, Britain and France had promised to aid Poland if it was invaded. Meanwhile, Hitler made a secret pact with Stalin, Russia's leader, for them to divide Poland's land between them if the Red Army from the east also invaded.

On September 1, 1939, a combined German aerial and ground attack force rolled across the Polish border. This blitzkrieg, or "lightning war," was unstoppable. Two days later, Britain and France declared war on Germany. By October 6, all of Poland was in German and Soviet hands.

During September, the British had sent an Expeditionary Force (the BEF), numbering one tenth of the total Allied defenders, to man France's eastern border. The Allies also planned to use blockades to stop Germany from getting iron ore via Norway, which would grind their war machine to a halt.

Before the Allies could do anything, Germany successfully occupied Denmark and Norway in April 1940. This was swiftly followed by the invasions of the neutral countries of the Netherlands, Belgium, and Luxembourg on May 10. Hitler's objective was to take northern France, from where he could demand Britain's surrender—the key to holding western Europe.

The speed of the invasion of the Low Countries surprised even the Germans.

THE BATTLE FOR FRANCE

By mid-May, the Germans had swept through Belgium and broken the French fortified line. Their plan to drive north toward the channel and trap the retreating Allied forces was working.

Britain's new prime minister, Winston Churchill, made plans for a possible evacuation. If the BEF was wiped out, Britain might have to surrender. Luckily, Hitler ordered a three-day halt to the advance, and the BEF escaped by the skin of its teeth from Dunkirk, in a huge fleet of ships that set out from England.

On June 22, 1940, with northern France occupied by Germany, the French agreed to install a puppet government in the rest of France. The Western Front was now just 21 miles (34 kilometers) from Britain's shore.

Paris was spared bombardment when it was surrendered on 14 June, 1940.

Although defeated, the rescue from Dunkirk kept the Allies' hopes alive.

THE BATTLE OF BRITAIN

In the summer of 1940, Hitler felt he had won the war. He couldn't understand why the British government was "*...set on fighting to the finish.*" To invade England was risky. Germany had only river barges with which to launch an amphibious assault and, before that, the British air force had to be neutralized.

Between July and October, waves of German bombers pounded Britain's air bases before turning their attention to its cities. Opposing the Luftwaffe were the brave pilots of the RAF in their Hurricanes and Spitfires. The Luftwaffe had lots of pilots but not enough planes, while Britain had the planes but lacked pilots. In the end, the invention of radar, a secret weapon, defeated the Luftwaffe and the invasion of Britain was postponed.

Britain's last remaining hope for the overthrow of the Nazis lay with the Russians but, in July 1941, Hitler launched an all-out assault to conquer the Soviet Union.

A spotter scans London's skies during the bombing of Britain, called the Blitz.

D-DAY

It had been quiet on the Western Front for two years. America had come into the war on the Allies' side, and the US troops, combined with British, Canadian, and French troops, had increased the army to more than 5,400,000. The German army, drained by the Eastern Front, numbered 1,500,000.

While no major land battles were fought, the strategic bombing of Germany had continued. The USAF raided in the daytime, and the RAF at night.

OPERATION OVERLORD

The Allies' grand plan to take Europe back would need more than 150,000 ground troops and an armada of landing craft and support ships. The chosen landing site was in Normandy, France. The operation would open with US and British paratroopers securing bridges leading to Normandy to prevent German reinforcements. Then amphibious assault craft would land troops and armor in waves during the crucial D-Day, to establish a base for the invasion of France.

A run of bad weather held D-Day back until June 6, 1944. The bad weather also prevented Allied bombing runs from taking out many of the beach defenses, which would have dire consequences for some US and Canadian units. Casualties for the entire operation were 10,000 men. After three days, the landing site was ready to push reinforcements to the offensive.

Of the five code-named beaches, Sword was the easiest to take, Omaha the most difficult.

The US Army, tasked with capturing Cherbourg to the south, found the high-hedged, or "bocage," terrain rough going and costly. The British didn't do much better with Caen to the north, where the Germans were stubbornly dug in.

THE FALAISE POCKET

The Allied breakout happened seven weeks after D-Day, when the US First Army launched an offensive into Brittany. The close-quarters infantry battles of Normandy gave way to tactics based on armored mobility, which the Germans couldn't hope to match. Their field commanders requested to fall back and form a defensive line along the

GIs reached Paris on August 25, 1944.

Seine River. Hitler was outraged and ordered an attack. This led to 50,000 Germans being encircled at Falaise. Their surrender meant that northwest France was lost. The road to Paris and the German border now lay open.

Operation Market Garden (September 17–25, 1944) was a bold British plan to use massed airborne troops to punch through from the Netherlands to the industrial heartland of Germany. It was a heroic failure.

Between August and December 1944, Allied troops battled hard to drive the Germans back inside their fortified border.

THE BATTLE OF THE BULGE

By winter 1944, Allied soldiers were stretched over an extended front that ran north all the way to Nijmegen, in the Netherlands. Hitler now launched a surprise counterattack to split the Allied line, and force them to seek a separate peace from Russia. This would safeguard Germany and allow them to continue the fight against the Soviets.

The Ardennes Offensive (December 16, 1944 to January 28, 1945) knocked the US lines back across an 80-mile (129-km) front causing a distinctive bulge on the map. The fighting was ferocious, but the Germans were held and forced back. There were 89,000 US casualties including 19,000 killed—the bloodiest US battle of World War II. The northern Rhine was the last remaining obstacle preventing the invasion of Germany and the ending of the war.

US soldiers in the Ardennes

John Bentley-Beard
Duel in the Skies—The Battle of Britain
September 27, 1940

OVER RAF NORTH WEALD IN ESSEX, HOME TO 249 SQUADRON, 1300 HOURS.

FIFTY PLUS BOMBERS, ONE HUNDRED PLUS FIGHTERS, OVER CANTERBURY AT 15,000 FEET, HEADING NORTHEAST...

THE ACTION ORDER CRACKLED OVER PILOT OFFICER BEARD'S HEADSET.

"...YOUR VECTOR IS NINE ZERO DEGREES, OVER."

THE 10 HURRICANES AND TWO SPITFIRES HAD BEEN CIRCLING – WAITING FOR INTERCEPT CO-ORDINATES. NOW THEY BANKED TO GO SOUTHWEST AT FULL POWER.

CROSSING OVER LONDON, THEY FLEW TOWARD THE BOMBER FORMATIONS.

THERE THEY ARE!

SCORES OF GERMAN HEINKELS SANDWICHED BETWEEN MESSERSCHMITT FIGHTERS WERE STACKED IN LAYERS THOUSANDS OF FEET (METERS) DEEP.

UNDER THE SQUADRON LEADER'S ORDERS, BEARD AND THE OTHERS SWUNG THEIR PLANES AROUND IN AN ARC AND DIVED.

ROAAAAAR!

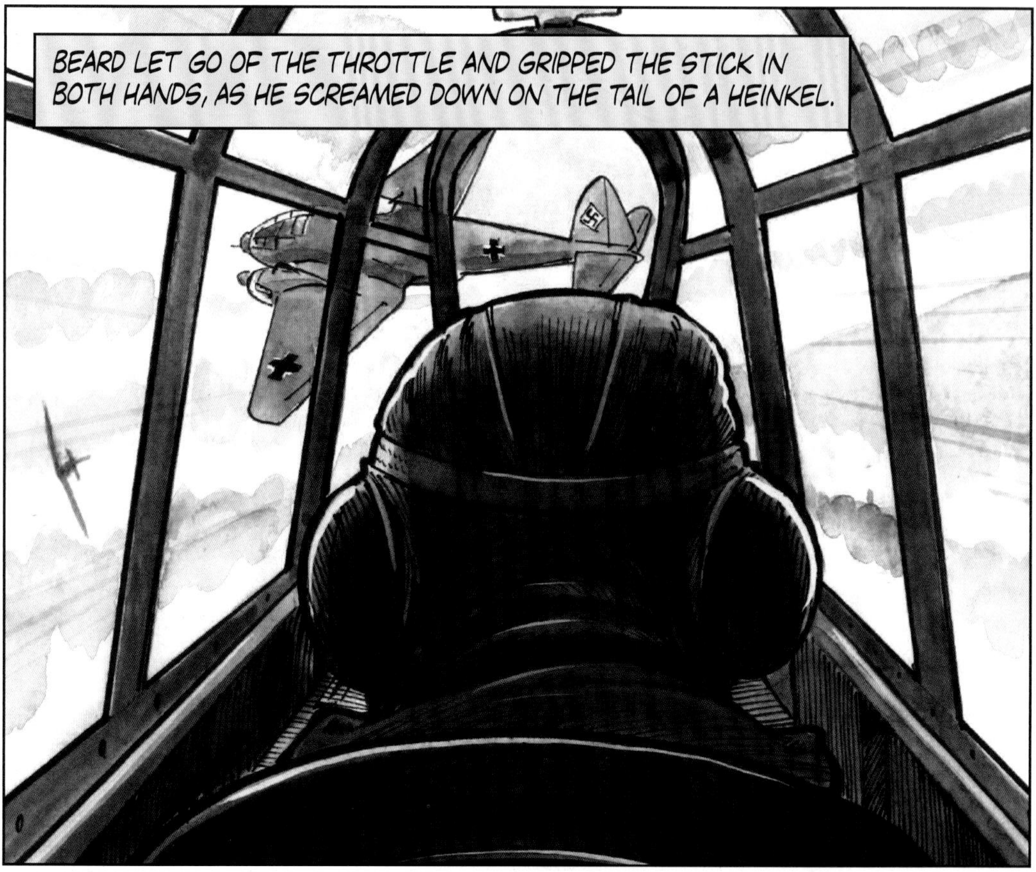
BEARD LET GO OF THE THROTTLE AND GRIPPED THE STICK IN BOTH HANDS, AS HE SCREAMED DOWN ON THE TAIL OF A HEINKEL.

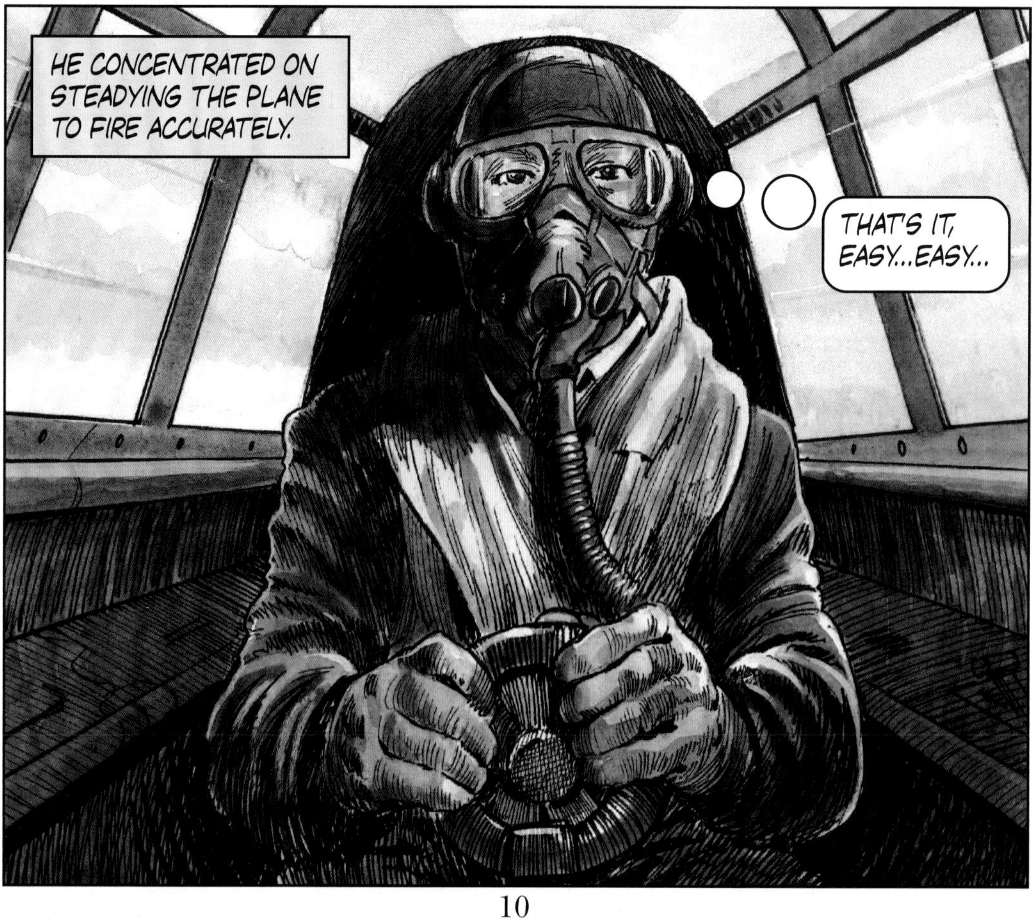
HE CONCENTRATED ON STEADYING THE PLANE TO FIRE ACCURATELY.
THAT'S IT, EASY...EASY...

THE HEINKEL GREW BIG IN HIS GUN SIGHT.

WHY DOESN'T HE MOVE?

BEARD MENTALLY JERKED THE STICK AS HE WOULD HAVE DONE IN THE ENEMY PILOT'S PLACE.

HE PRESSED THE TRIGGER. HIS PLANE TREMBLED AS HE SENT EIGHT STREAMS OF GUNFIRE, IN A TWO-SECOND BURST, TOWARD THE HEINKEL.

TAKK! TAKK! TAKK!

TAKK! TAKK! TAKK!

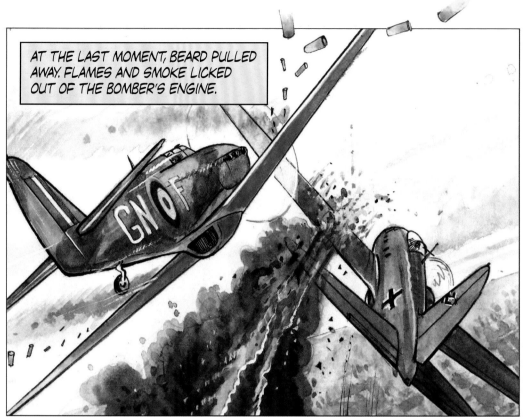

AT THE LAST MOMENT, BEARD PULLED AWAY. FLAMES AND SMOKE LICKED OUT OF THE BOMBER'S ENGINE.

BEARD PULLED BACK FIRMLY ON THE STICK, AND CLIMBED TO SEARCH FOR MORE TARGETS.

A DORNIER 17 BEING CHASED BY A HURRICANE ROARED ACROSS HIS FLIGHTLINE...

...AND TWO MESSERSCHMITTS WERE CHASING THAT HURRICANE.

THEY'RE FOCUSED ON THE HURRI' - THEY HAVEN'T SEEN ME.

PERFECT!

BEARD PRESSED HIS THUMB ON THE GUN BUTTON.

THE MACHINE GUNS SPAT OUT BULLETS AT 10 ROUNDS A SECOND.

TAKK!
TAKK!
TAKK!
TAKK!
TAKK!
TAKK!
TAKK!

HIS LINE OF FIRE ARCED OUT JUST AHEAD OF THE FIRST MESSERSCHMITT.

IT FLEW INTO THE BULLETS AND DISINTEGRATED.

GOTCHA!!

THE SECOND ENEMY PILOT IMMEDIATELY EXECUTED A LOOP AND A HALF ROLL TO AVOID THE BULLETS AND DEBRIS, AND GOT AWAY.

?!

WHAT SPECTACULAR FLYING – I HAVE TO HAND IT TO YOU!

A GLINT OF LIGHT CAUGHT HIS EYE. BEARD LOOKED QUICKLY IN HIS REARVIEW MIRROR.

MESSERSCHMITTS!

HE PULLED BACK HARD ON THE STICK. REAMS OF TRACER FIRE STREAMED JUST BELOW HIM.

THE MESSERSCHMITTS PULLED AWAY.

WHEW! THAT WAS CLOSE! I'D BETTER CHECK THE "OFFICE."

BEARD'S COCKPIT INSTRUMENTS SHOWED HE WAS LOW ON GAS AND AMMUNITION.

THAT'S IT - TIME TO HEAD FOR HOME.

BEARD'S NECK WAS STIFF FROM ALL THE STRESS. THE COCKPIT WAS BOILING HOT AND HE WAS SOAKED WITH SWEAT.

NEARLY ALL BEARD'S SQUADRON LANDED SAFELY. THEY HAD TAKEN OUT AT LEAST 30 ENEMY PLANES.

BUT IT WAS NOT OVER YET...

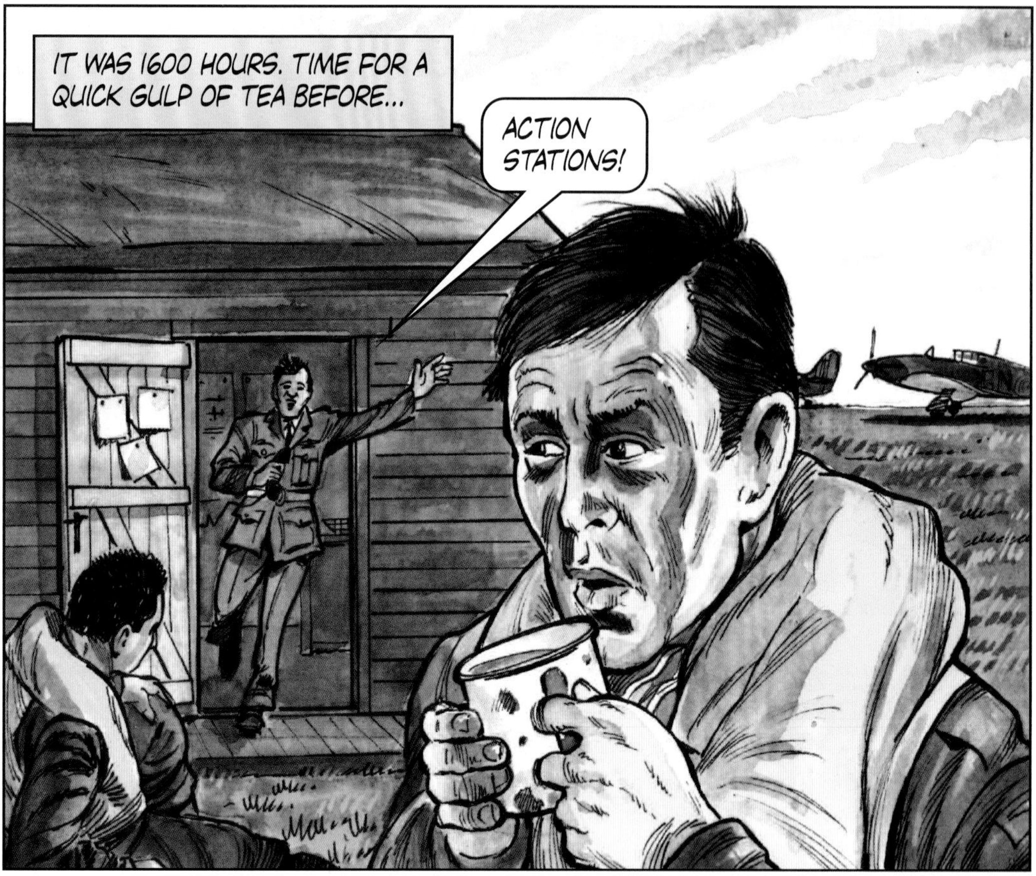
IT WAS 1600 HOURS. TIME FOR A QUICK GULP OF TEA BEFORE...
ACTION STATIONS!

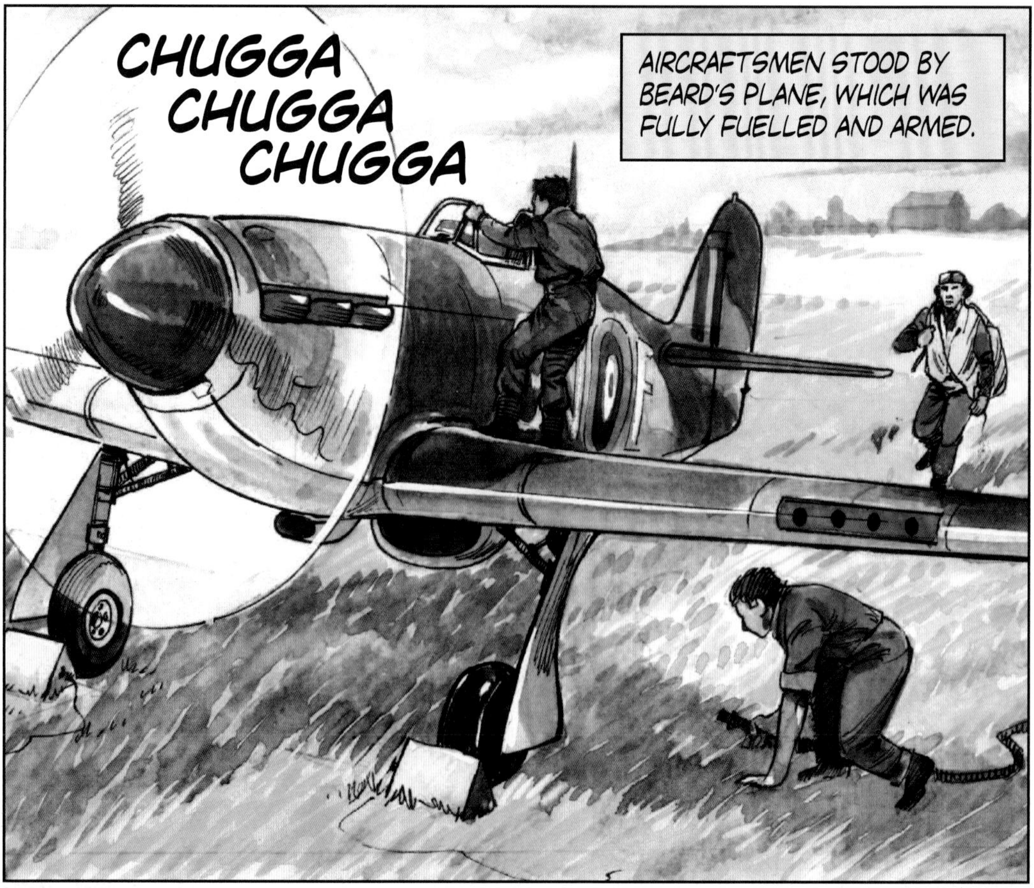
CHUGGA CHUGGA CHUGGA
AIRCRAFTSMEN STOOD BY BEARD'S PLANE, WHICH WAS FULLY FUELLED AND ARMED.

THE LINE OF ENEMY PLANES STRETCHED FROM HORIZON TO HORIZON. IN THIS BATTLE BEARD TOOK OUT A HEINKEL BUT HAD TO BALE OUT, INJURED, WHEN HIS PLANE GOT HIT BY ANTIAIRCRAFT FIRE.

JOHN BENTLEY-BEARD WAS ONE OF "THE FEW" – A SMALL NUMBER OF BRAVE PILOTS WHO HELPED WIN THE BATTLE OF BRITAIN. HE WAS AWARDED THE DISTINGUISHED FLYING MEDAL AND SURVIVED THE WAR.

THE END

Harold Baumgarten
SURVIVING OMAHA BEACH—D-DAY
JUNE 6, 1944

THE APPROACH TO DOG GREEN SECTOR, OMAHA BEACH, VIERVILLE, IN NORMANDY, FRANCE, 0640 HOURS.

A LANDING CRAFT LOADED WITH MEN OF 116TH INFANTRY REGIMENT, 29TH INFANTRY DIVISION - B COMPANY HAD JUST TAKEN A DIRECT HIT FROM AN ARTILLERY SHELL.

THE MEN IN THE LANDING CRAFT NEXT TO THEM, INCLUDING PRIVATE HAROLD BAUMGARTEN, WERE SHOWERED WITH WOOD, METAL, AND BLOOD.

AS THEIR RAMP WENT DOWN, A HAIL OF MACHINE GUN BULLETS POURED IN, GRAZING BAUMGARTEN'S HELMET AND KILLING THE SOLDIER IN FRONT OF HIM.

AARRRRGH!

DING!

COMPANIES A, B, C, AND D HAD BEEN TASKED WITH OPENING UP THE MAIN ROAD OUT – THE VIERVILLE DRAW – ON THE MOST HEAVILY-GUARDED SECTION OF OMAHA BEACH.

BAUMGARTEN JUMPED INTO WATER THAT WAS CHURNING WITH GUNFIRE.

GNNNNGH!

HIS TOES TOUCHED THE BOTTOM. HE BARELY KEPT HIS HEAD ABOVE THE WATER. AROUND HIM, SOME OF THE SHORTER SOLDIERS STRUGGLED WITH THEIR EQUIPMENT. SOME WERE PULLED UNDER OR WERE SHOT.

GASP!

BAUMGARTEN PLOWED FORWARD.

THE SURVIVORS EMERGED FROM THE OCEAN AND RAN ACROSS SAND STREWN WITH BODIES AND RAKED BY MACHINE GUN FIRE. THROUGH THE SMOKE, BAUMGARTEN COULD SEE HIS IMMEDIATE OBJECTIVE.

GASP! THE SEAWALL!

HE FELT HIS RIFLE KICK WHEN A BULLET SLAMMED INTO ITS RECEIVER.

HUH?!

AAAGH!

THWAP

THUNK

BAUMGARTEN TOOK SHELTER BEHIND A BEACH DEFENSE CALLED A HEDGEHOG. THE DEAD AND DYING MEN FROM "A" COMPANY, WHO HAD LANDED FIRST, LITTERED THE BEACH.

AAAGH – I'M HIT! MOTHER, HELP ME!

THE TIDE IS COMING IN FAST...

THE WATER SWIRLED AS BAUMGARTEN TOOK AIM AT THE LIGHT HE SPOTTED BOUNCING OFF A GERMAN HELMET ON THE BLUFF BEYOND.

HE FIRED.

CRACK!

THE MACHINE GUN FELL SILENT, BUT...

MY RIFLE - IT'S JAMMED!

GNNNNGH - COME ON!

HE USED HIS FOOT TO TRY TO FREE THE BOLT.

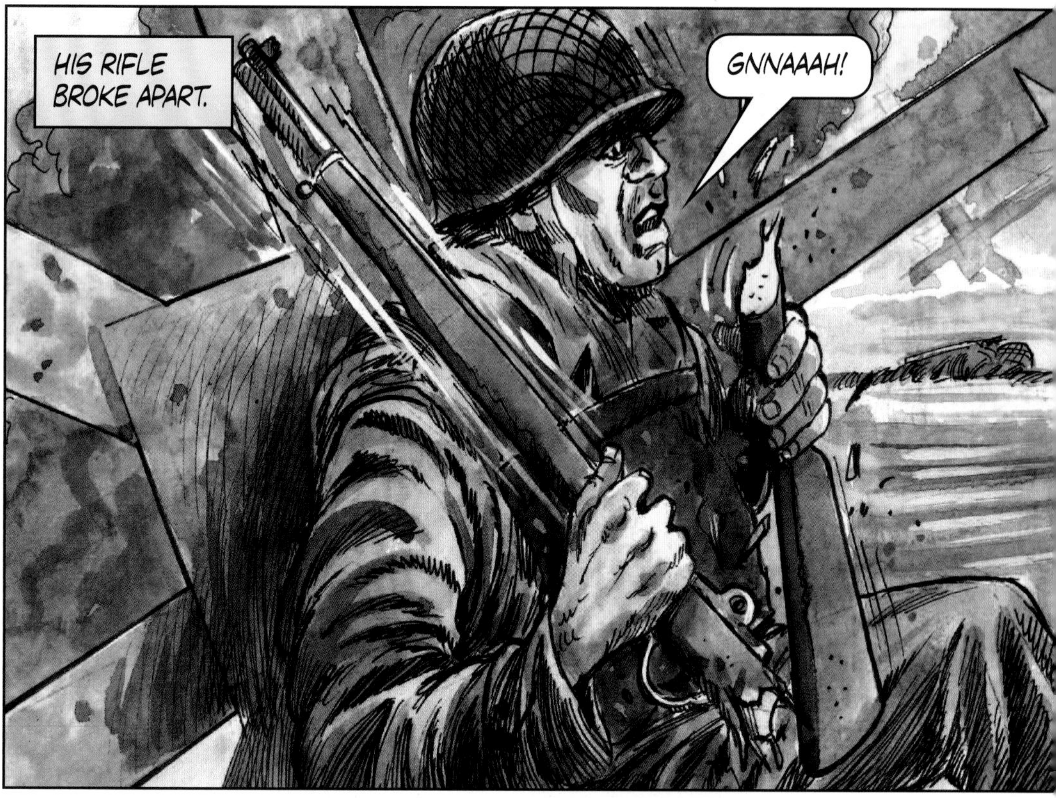
HIS RIFLE BROKE APART.
GNNAAAH!

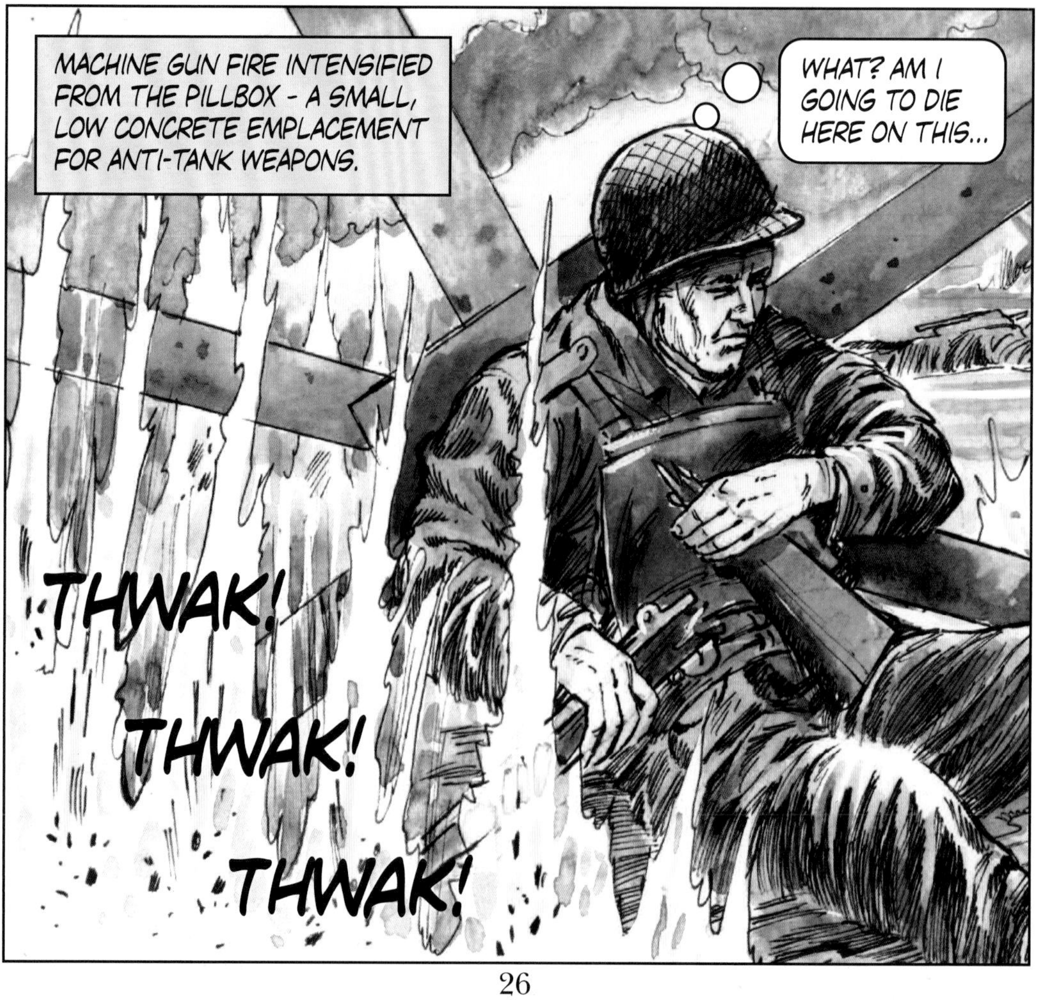
MACHINE GUN FIRE INTENSIFIED FROM THE PILLBOX - A SMALL, LOW CONCRETE EMPLACEMENT FOR ANTI-TANK WEAPONS.
WHAT? AM I GOING TO DIE HERE ON THIS...
THWAK!
THWAK!
THWAK!

BAM!

A MORTAR SHELL EXPLODED RIGHT IN FRONT OF HIM. BAUMGARTEN FELT AN IMPACT ON HIS JAW LIKE HE'D BEEN HIT WITH A BASEBALL BAT.

AAAAGH – MY FACE!

MANAGING TO STAY CONSCIOUS HE FELL FORWARD AND SLOPPED THE WOUND WITH DIRTY TIDE WATER.

HE FELT HIS CHEEK. THE LEFT UPPER JAW WAS GONE, HE COULD FEEL TEETH AND GUMS LYING ACROSS HIS TONGUE. A RAGGED PIECE OF FLESH HUNG OVER HIS LEFT EAR.

EVERYBODY'S GONE... WHEN WILL IT BE ME?

FROM A BUNKER THE GERMANS RAKED THE
BEACH WITH A 1,200-ROUNDS-PER-MINUTE
MACHINE GUN THEY CALLED THE "BONESAW."

DRRRRRRRRRR

BAD WEATHER HAD CAUSED THE ALLIED BOMBING RUNS TO MISS THIS
AND ALL THE OTHER GERMAN POSITIONS. MACHINE GUNS, MORTARS,
AND SNIPERS HAD 1ST BATTALION PINNED IN A MURDEROUS CROSSFIRE.

BAUMGARTEN POPPED THE CLIPS
ON HIS EQUIPMENT PACKS...

GOT TO GET TO
THAT WALL...

...AND CRAWLED FAST
AS BULLETS RIPPED UP
THE SAND AROUND HIM.

THWIP

THWIP

THWIP

THWIP

REACHING THE WALL HE GRABBED A LOOSE M1 RIFLE FROM A DEAD COMRADE AND HELPED OTHERS.

GOT TO GET OFF THIS BEACH. WHERE ARE OUR REINFORCEMENTS?

CROSSING THE WALL HE WAS YANKED BACK JUST IN TIME TO AVOID A BURST OF MACHINE GUN FIRE THAT TORE UP THE ROAD AHEAD.

NO YOU DON'T!

MEDIC!!

KEOW!

KEOW!

KEOW!

A MEDIC PINNED HIM DOWN AND APPLIED SULPHUR POWDER TO HIS FACE AS MORTAR FRAGMENTS AND BULLETS FLEW AROUND.

URRRGH...YOU MUST GET DOWN!

YOU'RE HURT NOW. AFTER I GET WOUNDED YOU CAN TAKE CARE OF ME!

COMPANY D - THE REINFORCEMENTS WITH HEAVY WEAPONS FOR DOG GREEN, HAD LANDED OUT OF POSITION DUE TO SMOKE. THEY WERE MISSING EQUIPMENT AND HAD TAKEN MANY CASUALTIES, BUT...

COME ON, WE'VE GOT SOME FIGHTING TO DO!

BY MID-MORNING THEY HOOKED UP WITH OTHER SURVIVORS AND, LED BY THEIR COLONELS, MADE THEIR WAY THROUGH THE MINEFIELDS AND OFF THE BEACH.

THE INVASION HAD STARTED.

BY PLACING EXPLOSIVES AND CALLING IN ARTILLERY FIRE FROM DESTROYERS THAT CAME CLOSE INSHORE, THE GERMAN POSITIONS WERE GRADUALLY TAKEN OUT.

BADOOM!

BY DAY'S END MORE THAN 2,000 BODIES, ALONG WITH DISCARDED EQUIPMENT AND BURNING VEHICLES, LITTERED THE SHORE - TESTAMENT TO THE SACRIFICE AT OMAHA BEACH.

BAUMGARTEN WAS WOUNDED FOUR MORE TIMES BEFORE HE WAS EVACUATED OUT OF NORMANDY.

THE END

Alexander A. Drabik
Capturing the Bridge at Remagen – The Invasion of Germany

1530 HOURS, MARCH 7, 1945, REMAGEN, WEST BANK OF THE RHINE, GERMANY.

ON CAPTURING REMAGEN, GENERAL COURTNEY H. HODGES, COMMANDER OF THE US FIRST ARMY, HAD BEEN ASTONISHED TO FIND THE LUDENDORFF BRIDGE STILL INTACT, BUT...

...I JUST FOUND OUT, SIR – THE GERMANS PLAN TO BLOW THE BRIDGE AT 1600 HOURS.

ORDER UP SOME SMOKE COVER – WE'RE GOING TO TAKE THAT BRIDGE!

IT WAS A GAMBLE, AND AGAINST ORDERS, BUT HODGES FIGURED IT WAS WORTH THE RISK.

SERGEANT ALEXANDER A DRABIK, ALONG WITH THE OTHER SOLDIERS OF ABLE COMPANY, PREPARED TO STEP OUT ONTO THE BRIDGE.

KEEP LOW, BOYS!

PEOW! PEOW! PEOW! PEOW!

MACHINE GUN FIRE FROM DEFENSIVE TOWERS PEPPERED THE APPROACH.

SUDDENLY...

BOOOM!

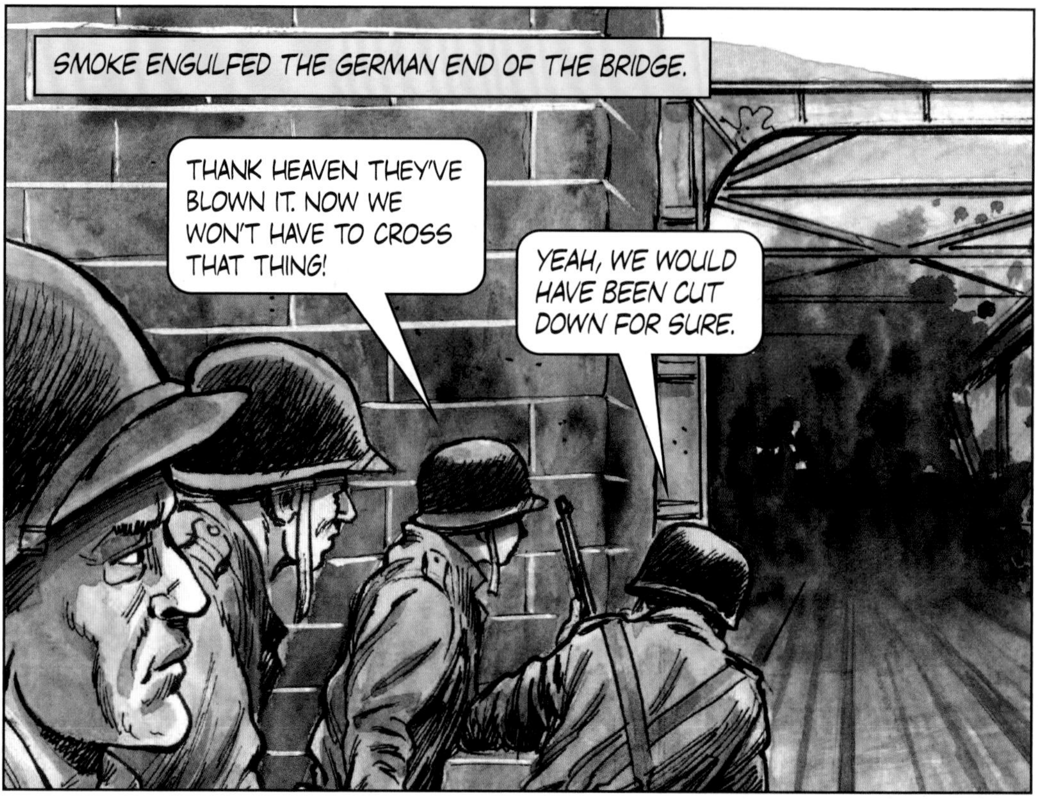
SMOKE ENGULFED THE GERMAN END OF THE BRIDGE.
THANK HEAVEN THEY'VE BLOWN IT. NOW WE WON'T HAVE TO CROSS THAT THING!
YEAH, WE WOULD HAVE BEEN CUT DOWN FOR SURE.

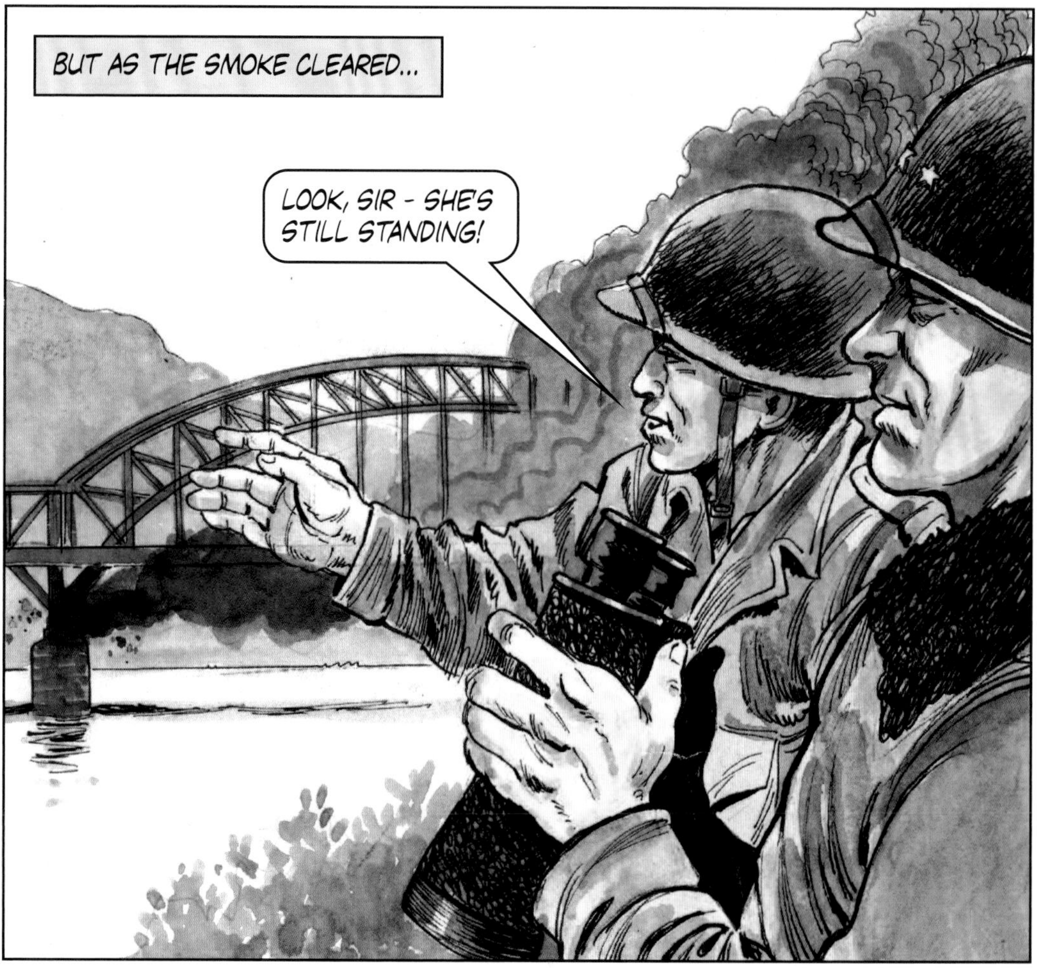
BUT AS THE SMOKE CLEARED...
LOOK, SIR - SHE'S STILL STANDING!

FROM ONE OF THE WEST TOWERS LIEUTENANT CARL TIMMERMANN COULD SEE DOWN THE LENGTH OF THE BRIDGE. THE GERMANS WERE PREPARING TO SET MORE CHARGES.

THE TRACK BED'S HOLED BUT IF WE USE THE WALKWAYS WE CAN GET ACROSS!

TIMMERMANN LED HIS MEN.

PLATOON, LET'S GO!

SHARP FIRE FROM A GUN TOWER MADE TIMMERMANN DUCK DOWN.

PEOW!

PEOW!

PEOW!

A PERSHING TANK TURNED ITS GUN TOWARDS THE TOWER AND BLASTED.

BOOOM!

THE TOWER WENT QUIET.

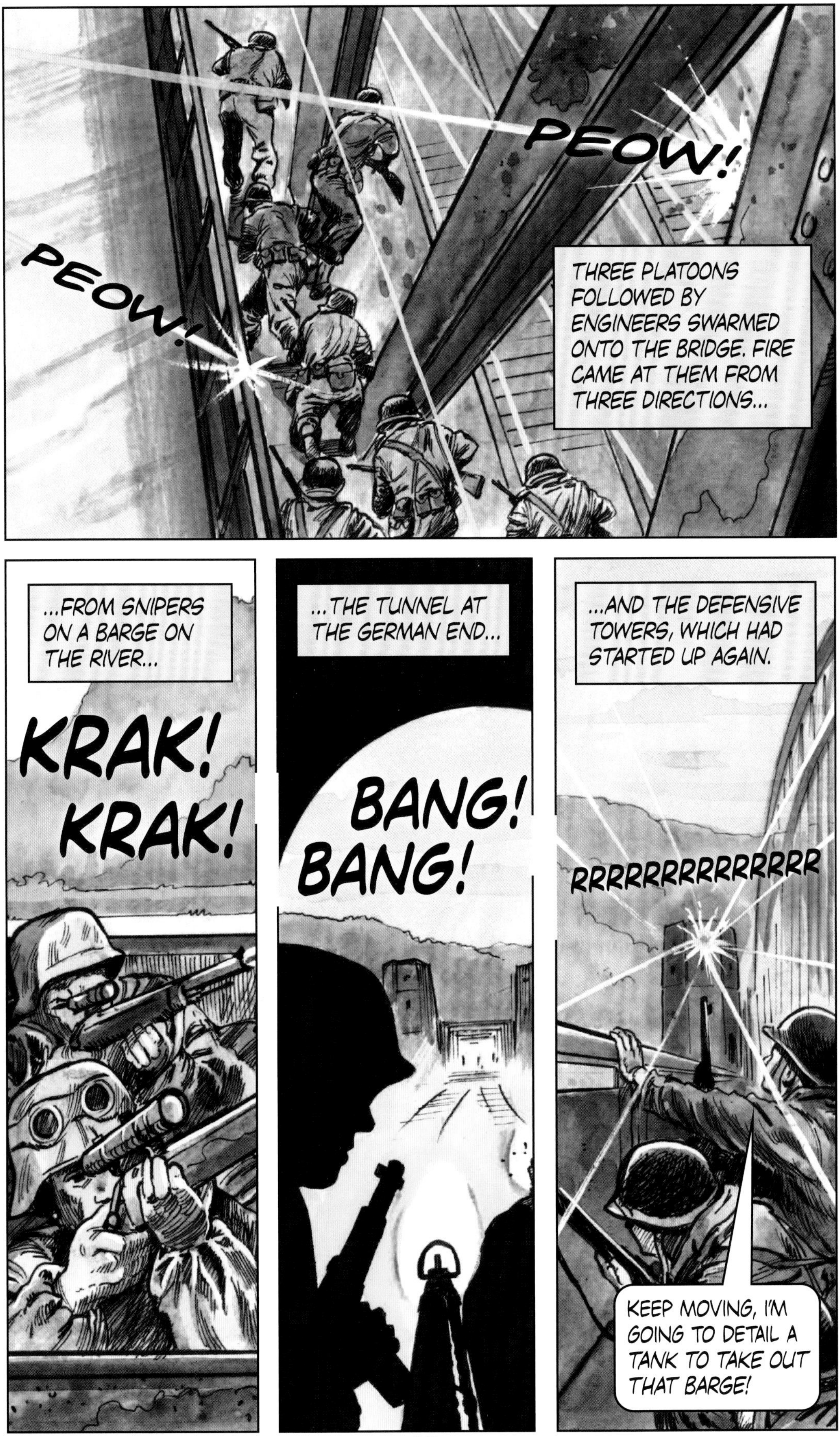
PEOW!
PEOW!
THREE PLATOONS FOLLOWED BY ENGINEERS SWARMED ONTO THE BRIDGE. FIRE CAME AT THEM FROM THREE DIRECTIONS...
...FROM SNIPERS ON A BARGE ON THE RIVER...
KRAK! KRAK!
...THE TUNNEL AT THE GERMAN END...
BANG! BANG!
...AND THE DEFENSIVE TOWERS, WHICH HAD STARTED UP AGAIN.
RRRRRRRRRRRRR
KEEP MOVING, I'M GOING TO DETAIL A TANK TO TAKE OUT THAT BARGE!

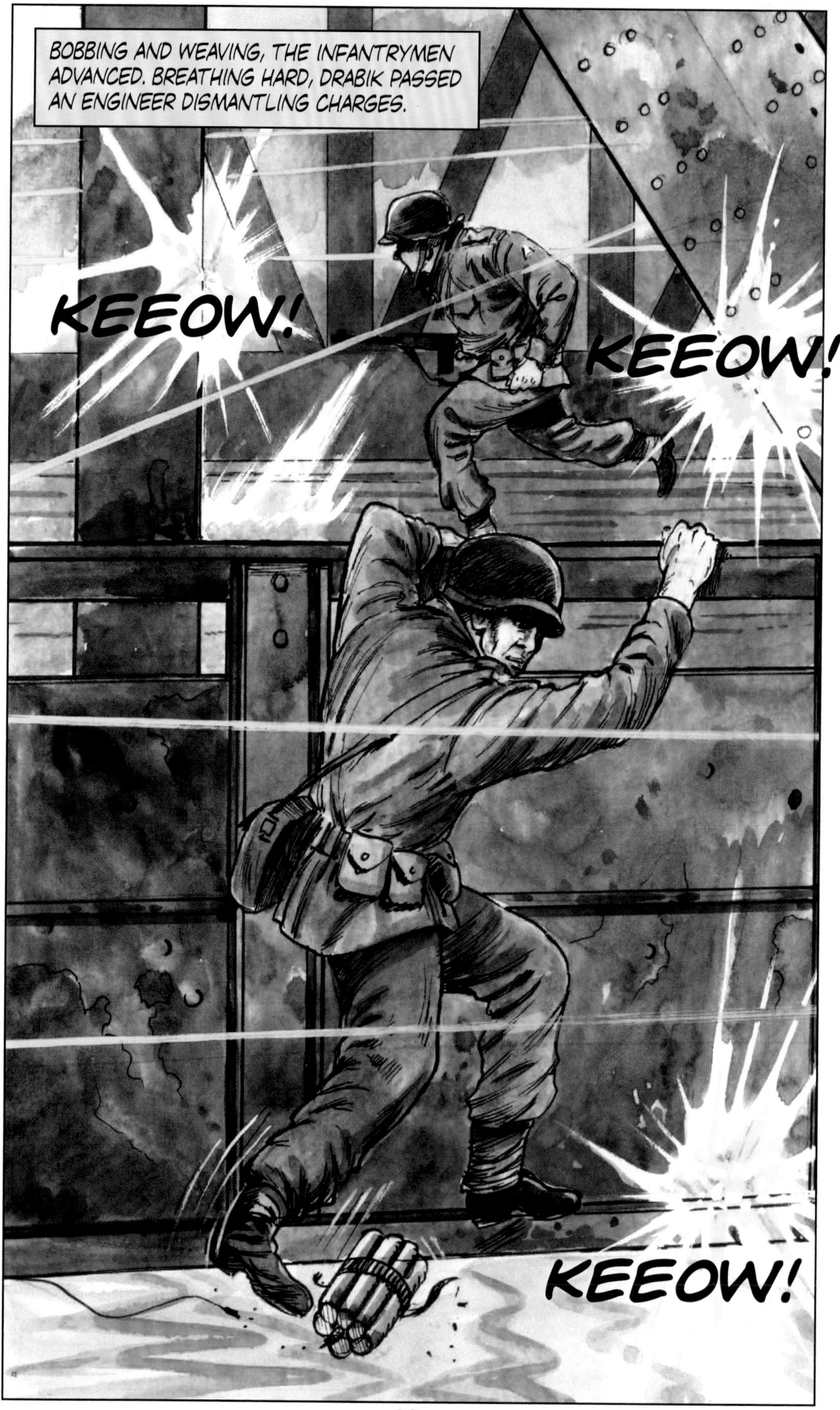

BOBBING AND WEAVING, THE INFANTRYMEN ADVANCED. BREATHING HARD, DRABIK PASSED AN ENGINEER DISMANTLING CHARGES.
KEEOW!
KEEOW!
KEEOW!

THE BARGE ON THE RIVER DISINTEGRATED IN A FLARE OF HIGH EXPLOSIVE.

FOOOM!

BOOOM!

DELISIO, TAKE OUT THE TOWER!

YES SIR!

AS DELISIO REACHED THE BASE OF THE TOWER, BULLETS RICOCHETED AROUND HIM.

SIR, YOU'RE HIT!

HE FELT FOR BLOOD.

NO, NO, I'M ALRIGHT!

HE LED HIS MEN UP THE TOWER STEPS.

THAT'S IT - HANDS UP, SCHNELL! SCHNELL!*

*QUICKLY! QUICKLY!

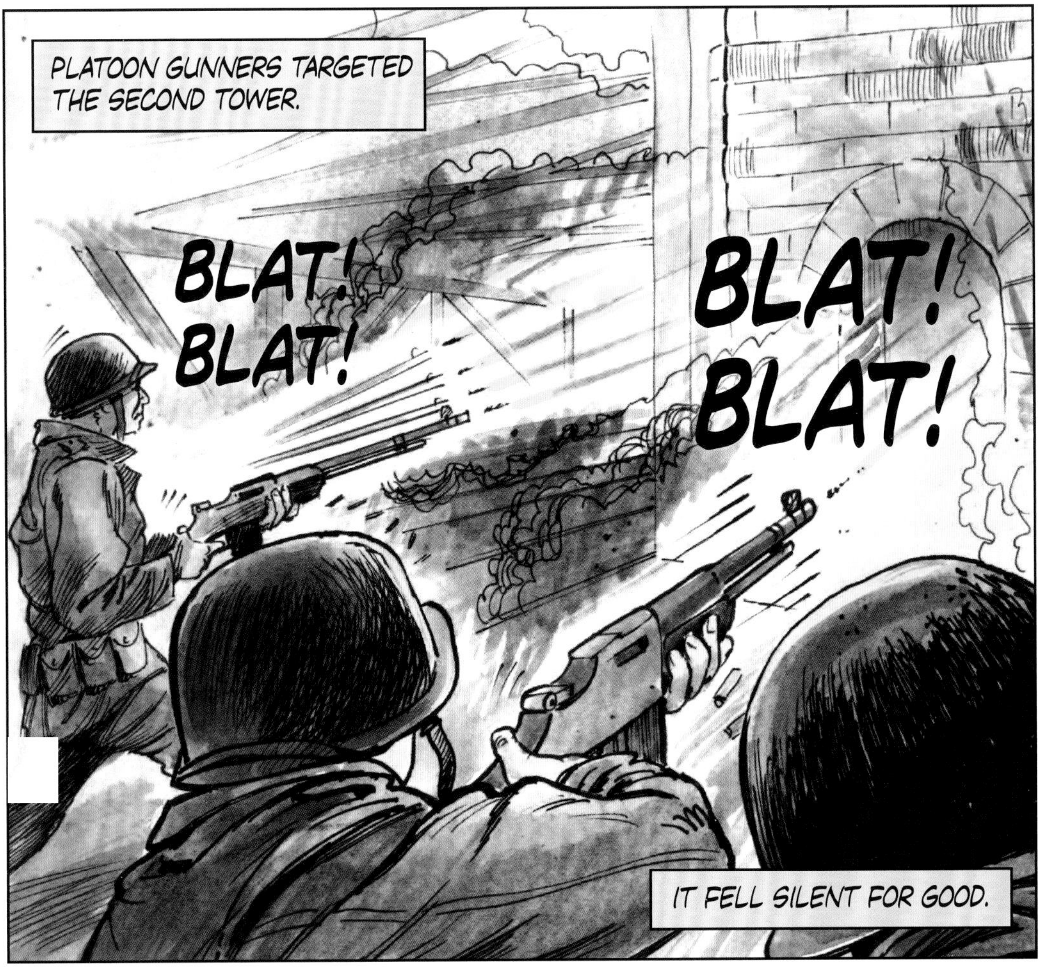
PLATOON GUNNERS TARGETED THE SECOND TOWER.
BLAT! BLAT!
BLAT! BLAT!
IT FELL SILENT FOR GOOD.

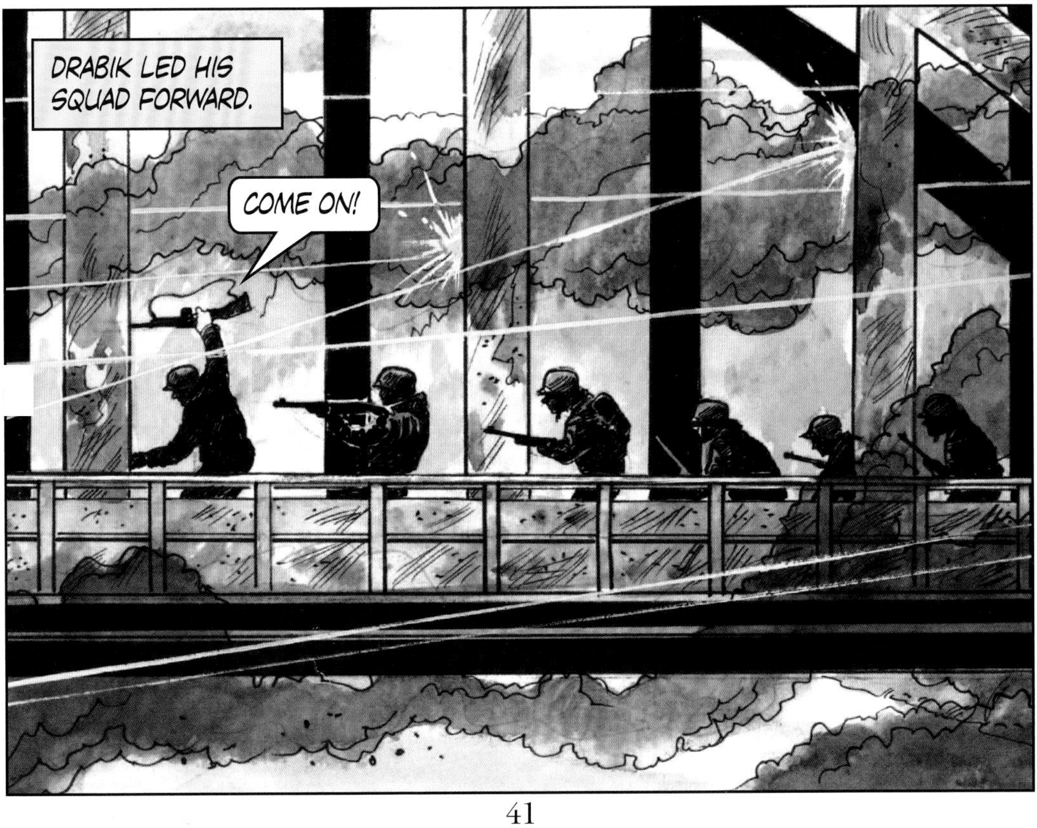
DRABIK LED HIS SQUAD FORWARD.
COME ON!

DODGING SHOTS FROM THE TUNNEL, DRABIK SPRINTED LEFT DOWN THE RIVER ROAD, CLOSELY FOLLOWED BY THE REST OF HIS SQUAD.

KRAK!

KRAK!

BANG!

WHEW! WE GOT IT!

DRABIK WAS THE FIRST MAN ACROSS - THE FIRST INVADER TO REACH THE EAST BANK OF THE RHINE RIVER SINCE THE TIME OF NAPOLEON.

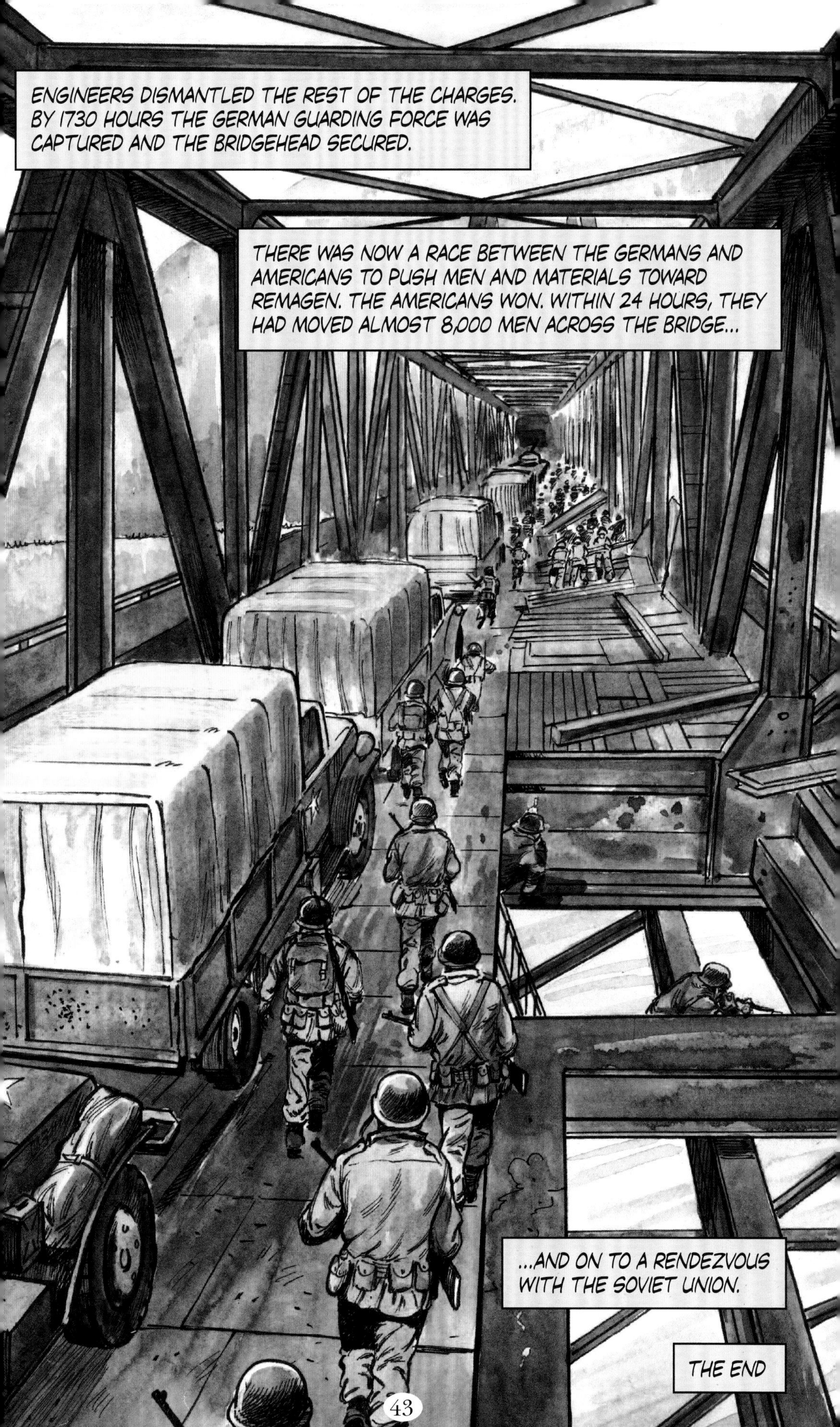
ENGINEERS DISMANTLED THE REST OF THE CHARGES. BY 1730 HOURS THE GERMAN GUARDING FORCE WAS CAPTURED AND THE BRIDGEHEAD SECURED.
THERE WAS NOW A RACE BETWEEN THE GERMANS AND AMERICANS TO PUSH MEN AND MATERIALS TOWARD REMAGEN. THE AMERICANS WON. WITHIN 24 HOURS, THEY HAD MOVED ALMOST 8,000 MEN ACROSS THE BRIDGE...
...AND ON TO A RENDEZVOUS WITH THE SOVIET UNION.
THE END

VICTORY IN EUROPE

The Eastern and Western fronts met at the River Elbe on April 25, 1945.

In early March 1945, the German forces were in a hopeless position as they tried to fight off invading armies on both sides. It would take the Western Allies just five weeks to capture the north, center, and south of western Germany, while the Red Army battled through former Poland and encircled Berlin.

FINAL ACT

Hitler's planned 1000-year Reich (empire) had lasted just 12 years. He first blamed his generals for all the military reversals, then his own people for lacking the will to gain victory. On April 30, as Soviet artillery shells rained down on his bunker, Adolf Hitler committed suicide.

Command passed to Grand Admiral Dönitz, who quickly made plans for most of the German forces to surrender to the West, whom he believed would be more humane. On May 7, surrender documents were signed at US General Dwight D. Eisenhower's headquarters in Rheims, France. The war in Europe was over at last.

Hitler's death as reported by the US Army in the Stars and Stripes

ATROCITY

In 1941, the Allies became aware that the Germans were building concentration camps in occupied Poland. It had begun with the forced settling of Polish Jews into ghettos within major cities. Nazi ideology held that pure-bred Germans were a "master race" and, during Hitler's rise to power, Jewish people and other minorities had been victimized, robbed of their human rights, even killed. Between 1941 and 1945, this policy was taken to its chilling logical conclusion.

A war reporter sits by the ashes of the dead at Buchenwald.

The true horror of the Nazi concentration camps was revealed when US troops liberated Buchenwald in Weimar, east-central Germany, on April 11, 1945. It is estimated that 9 million people were murdered by the Nazis in these camps. Six million of those victims were Jewish.

AFTERMATH

Hitler's bid to gain Lebensraum had resulted in Armageddon for his homeland and much of the rest of Europe. Major cities in many countries lay in ruins from bombing or ground fighting. Tens of millions of people had been killed. The war effort had left countries such as Britain virtually penniless, and it was up to the United States to loan money to help rebuild western Europe.

Germany itself was divided into four— to be occupied by the United States, Britain, and France in the west, and the Soviet Union in the east. Never again would the ambitions of a dictator be allowed to tear Europe apart.

US troops move through a ruined town in south-west Germany during the final weeks of the war.

GLOSSARY

Allied forces The joint military forces fighting against Germany and Japan during World War II

amphibious The ability to carry out activity on both water and land

annexed One territory becoming a part of another through the other's seizure of the previously independent territory

armada A grouping of ships used during times of war

Blitz, the The term used for the German air raids on Britain during World War II

blitzkrieg The use of intense military action with the intention of bringing about a quick, favorable outcome

casualties Those in hostile engagements who die, are captured, or go missing

evacuation The quick removal of a group of people, out of danger, to a safe area

expeditionary force A grouping of military personnel specified for dispatch on foreign soil

fortified Strengthened to support a better defense

Heinkel A type of German aircraft used during World War II

A bombed-out London street in 1940

Lebensraum An area of land, or living space, that a nation believes is necessary for its proper development

Low Countries Belgium, the Netherlands, and Luxembourg

Luftwaffe The German Air Force

Messerschmitt A type of German aircraft used during World War II

Nazi A person who followed the ideals and actions of Adolf Hitler; a member of the National Socialist German Workers' Party

neutral Impartial; not favoring either side of a conflict

neutralized The destruction of a threat

paratroopers Soldiers in an area of the military specifically trained for parachuting

postponed Held off until a later time when the conditions become more favorable

puppet government A government put in place and controlled by a foreign authority

RAF Abbreviation for Royal Air Force, the air force of Great Britain

rendezvous To meet up with another person or group at a specified time and place

tactics Plan of action to bring about a specific result

tracers Chemical trails from ammunition that help shooters correct their aim

USAF Abbreviation for United States Air Force

vector The direction of travel to be taken by an aircraft

A US infantryman takes a German officer prisoner in the Ardennes in 1944.

INDEX

A

Allied forces 4-7, 28, 44
America 6, 43
Ardennes Offensive 7, 47
Austria 4

B

Baumgarten, Harold 20-31
Belgium 4, 5
Bentley-Beard, John 8-19
Berlin 44
Blitz, the 5
Britain 4-5, 8, 19, 45
British Expeditionary Force 4-5
Brittany 7
Buchenwald 44

C

Caen 6
Canada 6
Cherbourg 6
Churchill, Winston 5
concentration camps 44
Czechoslovakia 4

D

D-Day 6-7, 20
Dönitz, Grand Admiral 44
Drabik, Alexander A. 32-43

E

Eastern Front 6
Eisenhower, Dwight D. 44
Elbe River 44
England 5

F

Falaise 7
France 4-7, 20, 44-45

G

Germany 4-7, 32, 44-45

H

Heinkel aircraft 9-11, 19
Hitler, Adolf 4-5, 7, 44-45
Hurricane aircraft 5, 8, 13

L

London 5, 9, 46
Luftwaffe 5
Luxembourg 4

M

Messerschmitt aircraft 9, 13-14, 16-17

N

Nazi 5, 44
Netherlands 4, 6
Nijmegen 7
Normandy 6, 7, 20, 31
Norway 4

O

Omaha Beach 6, 20-21, 31
Operation Market Garden 7

P

Paris 5, 7
Poland 4, 44

R

Red Army 4, 44
Rhine River 7, 32, 42
Royal Air Force 5, 6
Russia 4, 5, 7

S

Seine River 7
Soviet Union 4-5, 7, 43-45, 47
Spitfire aircraft 5, 8
Stalin 4
Sword Beach 6

T

Timmermann, Karl 35-36

U

United States 6-7, 32, 44-45, 47
United States Air Force 6

W

Western Front 5-6